T0159420

PAWS

for

THOUGHT

Assistance Dogs Australia is a national charity that provides freedom and independence to children and adults living with disability. We train Labrador and Golden Retriever puppies through a two-year, internationally accredited program, teaching them up to 50 specialised commands to provide support and increased mobility for their owner.

These incredible dogs aptly learn how to become an extra pair of hands—from loading a washing machine, opening and closing doors, pressing the pedestrian button at lights—to improving communication, empathy and motor skills of a child diagnosed with autism. The physical support our trained dogs provide lasts their 8- to 10-year working life.

Our Assistance Dogs make a dramatic difference for their owners in other ways too; their wagging tail and unconditional love relieving social isolation and increasing their owners' long-term independence to give them a better quality of life.

To date we have placed over 160 assistance dogs, free of charge, across Australia. Your support through purchasing this book will enable us to continue this very im-paw-tant work and transform the lives of people with disability.

We are grateful for the generous support of Assistance Dogs Australia and Christine Bernasconi of bernasconiphotography.com in capturing these beautiful images.

PAWS

for

THOUGHT

Finding the meaning of life takes years,
but innocence in life can be found every day.

'Yeah OK, so I might look a little silly,
but it's Christmas—'tis the silly season after all!'

'Don't worry, I'm not hurting him—we're just playing.'

———————

'Everywhere I go, here I am!.'

'Waiting and watching brings wisdom—
I listen and I learn and I do so without resentment.
Patience is golden.'

'So you were serious when you said just the one treat?
You don't have just one more?'

Life can be scary but don't ever let a shadow of your former self prevent you from achieving greatness.

'I know you wish you were me right now, huh?
Just sitting back, chilling, getting my daily dose of Vitamin D.'

*'I know what you're thinking ...
you really want to take me for a walk don't you?'*

The world is round but everyone in the world has a different
view so appreciate everyone's unique outlook.

*'We might sleep a lot but when we're awake
you have our love and attention unconditionally.'*

*'That's my sister for you—
always giving you the best angle!'*

17

Puppies are beautiful animals,
but true beauty is when the beauty they show comes from within.

'What's that smell?
You haven't got any of that seafood kibble have you?
It's my favourite!'

*Friends come and go in life, but sleep soundly knowing
family will always have your back.*

Imitation is the greatest form of flattery—if someone emulates
you, be gracious and carry on being you.

'We might not be the best at our job right now,
but we promise we're going to give it our all to make you proud.'

'Sure I might be a different colour to my brothers and sisters,
but the amount of love, patience and loyalty I show is just the same.'

The paws of a pup make our hearts melt with devotion.

'It's the bandana isn't it? It scares everyone!'

'I reckon I've got one of the best gigs in town—
my paws change people's lives!'

Life can be stressful sometimes,
but don't ever let it stop you from having fun!

29

'I wonder if I'll get in trouble for chewing apart those slippers?'

'It takes a keen eye to decorate the tree and make it look good—
you have to get the tinsel just right!'

'I usually love water, but the beach? It seems
a bit scary—what's with all the waves?'

'Yuuuummmmy!
That was the best brisket bone EVER!'

'Whoa, this sand can get s-l-i-p-p-e-r-y!'

'Intruder, intruder! Can you please get this pup
his own bed?'

'YES! First one back on dry land again! Haha, I might
be the smallest but it looks like I'm the fastest!'

'I enjoy my job but what I really love is,
at the end of the day, just lying in bed playing with my toys.'

Some things you carry around in life might be uncomfortable,
but don't ever hesitate to lighten the load
and ask for help.

'This photo shoot is tiring! 10 seconds more,
then I'm going to play, okay?'

'Shh ... don't move. I think I just spotted
Oscar the cat ...'

Never give up the fight for something you want; if you're meant
to have it, you will, but if you lose, don't forget there are many
more battles to be won.

*'What do you think? Would you back
me at the next Melbourne Cup?'*

'These two are my besties;
I will always have their back. Loyalty is rare, if you find it,
nurture it and never let it go.'

A dog holds its paws out to you its entire life;
don't forget to reward with kindness.

'People do say my brother's not the brightest pup in the pack.
Don't worry, he'll eventually work out that you don't eat trees!'

'I could have sworn I left my bone right here!
If that brother of mine has taken it again ...'

Work hard, play hard; but at the end of a long hard day
don't feel guilty about putting your feet up!

'When life seems uncertain I know I'll be okay. I might get scared
but my courage brings me one step closer to fearlessness.'

Finding the meaning of life takes years,
but innocence in life can be found every day.

'Sorry, but it's him or me ... it's not that hard.
Who's cuter, really?'

If you're courageous enough to take the road less travelled in life, hold your head high and welcome success.

'No, I am not moving!
I'm staying right here until Santa comes.'

'What do I do now? Hop in?'

Whether you have a close family or not,
there will always be someone's shoulder
somewhere you can lean on.

Life gets busy;
we all grow up, but don't forget to make time for the people
you love the most.

'Chest out, head up and strut!
It might take all day but I will nail this walk!'

He might not always be at the top of the class
but true success comes from dedication to never stop trying.

'I love Christmas but taking down the decorations
has to be the best part!'

*Never lose sight of the bigger picture, but most importantly
never forget to embrace each day—
run, laugh, dance and live in the moment.*

'Hehe ... this is the best! I knew you guys would love it!'

'Make sure you get the best angle—
I really want to make the front cover this month.'

Take time to appreciate life;
look up, look around, treasure the moments you have
and love the life you live.

*'How long do you think we'll have to wait?
I can't wait to get working again.'*

*'Although my days are packed full of things to do,
I love going to sleep at night knowing how much I matter.'*

*The sincerity in the eyes of a puppy communicates every level
of emotion; in moments of silence, take notice of one's eyes.*

'We run like it's our last chase.
We play like we won't see our friend for a long time.
We live in the moment.'

'Yes, this is not the most comfortable position but I'm really
tired! I just need to s-l-e-e-p.'

Dogs make us appreciate what really matters in life—
love, affection, loyalty and family.

'I can't wait to grow up and help somebody in a wheelchair one day.'

'What a day! My trainers taught me so many new things.
I'm excited about my job but a little scared too—
I hope I'll make them proud.'

If the struggle seems too hard, remember why you kept holding on.
Don't ever give up on your dreams.

*'Let's go. Last one back to the car has to do 100 push-ups
and 50 puppy squats!'*

Life flies by so quickly, don't neglect to take time out for yourself.
Reconnect and appreciate the silence.

'Are you sure we can't go out? I've got my ID!'

"I bet you know what's coming ...
it's time for a big, wet, cuddly puppy hug!"

Sometimes life brings sadness,
but happiness and success will always triumph.

'Hurry up please, I want to go and play.
And this pose is really hurting my neck!'

'I know my ears look funny when I run
but I've got to beat my brothers; there is no way I'm settling for leftovers!'

We may not always be confident in life
but never be afraid to look around for guidance.

'Water ... sand ... and a soggy ball—
my idea of puppy heaven.'

'Sailing looked fun but now I'm on board, I'm not so sure.'

Dream big, keep your eye on the prize;
do all that you need to do to bring you the happiness you deserve.

Take pleasure in the simple things in life—
unleash your curiosity and your imagination and creativity will flow.

'Sailing is definitely no run in the dog park. I'm out of here!'

'This looks like the perfect hiding spot!
Shh ... Don't tell anyone I'm here.'

Sleeping is a dog's bliss. Take time to find your own bliss.

From our family to yours—
Merry Christmas and may you enjoy a safe, happy and
healthy New Year!

First published in 2015 by New Holland Publishers Pty Ltd
London • Sydney • Auckland

The Chandlery, Unit 009, 50 Westminister Bridge Road London SE1 7QY United Kingdom
1/66 Gibbes Street Chatswood NSW 2067 Australia
218 Lake Road Northcote Auckland New Zealand

www.newhollandpublishers.com

A record of this book is held at the British Library and the National Library of Australia.

ISBN 9781742576350

Managing Director: Fiona Schultz
Publisher: Diane Ward
Project Editor: Susie Stevens
Designer: Andrew Quinlan
Photographs: Christine Bernasconi of bernasconiphotography.com
Production Director: Olga Dementiev
Printer: Toppan Leefung Printing Ltd (China)

Christine Bernasconi
p h o t o g r a p h y
bernasconiphotography.com

10 9 8 7 6 5 4 3 2 1

Keep up with New Holland Publishers on Facebook
www.facebook.com/NewHollandPublishers

US $9.99
UK £7.99

Assistance Dogs
Australia